# MAKING MOVIES

# Movie Stunts and Special Effects

by Geoffrey M. Horn

GARETH**STEVENS**
GS
P U B L I S H I N G
A Member of the WRC Media Family of Companies

Please visit our Web site at: www.garethstevens.com
For a free color catalog describing Gareth Stevens Publishing's
list of high-quality books and multimedia programs, call
1-800-542-2595 (USA) or 1-800-387-3178 (Canada).
Gareth Stevens Publishing's fax: (414) 332-3567.

Library of Congress Cataloging-in-Publication Data

Horn, Geoffrey M.
    Movie stunts and special effects / by Geoffrey M. Horn.
      p. cm. — (Making movies)
    Includes bibliographical references and index.
    ISBN-10: 0-8368-6840-4 — ISBN-13: 978-0-8368-6840-1 (lib. bdg.)
    1. Stunt performers—Juvenile literature.  2. Cinematography—Special effects—
Juvenile literature.  I. Title.  II. Series: Horn, Geoffrey M. Making movies.
  PN1995.9.S7H67   2007
  791.4302'8—dc22                                2006010498

This edition first published in 2007 by
**Gareth Stevens Publishing**
A Member of the WRC Media Family of Companies
330 West Olive Street, Suite 100
Milwaukee, WI 53212 USA

This edition copyright © 2007 by Gareth Stevens, Inc.

Concept: Sophia Olton-Weber
Managing Editor: Valerie J. Weber
Art direction and design: Tammy West
Picture research: Diane Laska-Swanke

Photo credits:  Cover, pp. 17 (right), 25 Warner Brothers/Photofest; p. 5
First National Pictures Inc./Photofest; pp. 8, 9, 19, 23, 24 © Everett Collection;
p. 11 Lucasfilm Ltd./Twentieth Century Fox Film Corp./Photofest; p. 12
Photofest; p. 14 Paramount Pictures/Photofest; p. 17 (left) © AP Images; p. 27
© Columbia/courtesy Everett Collection; p. 28 © New Line/courtesy Everett
Collection; p. 29 Walt Disney Pictures/Photofest

Printed in the United States of America

1 2 3 4 5 6 7 8 9 10 09 08 07 06

# Contents

Cover: A dazzling web of special effects made
*Spider-Man 2* a box-office smash in 2004.

# Monster Hits

On June 3, 1922, a very odd item appeared on the front page of the *New York Times*. The newspaper article described a talk that Sir Arthur Conan Doyle gave to a group of famous magicians. Doyle was the author of the *Sherlock Holmes* detective stories. He had also written a book called *The Lost World*.

Doyle showed the magicians part of an unfinished movie. In the film, dinosaurs roamed through an ancient jungle. They played. They made love. They fought and killed each other. The magicians didn't know what to think. Were the dinosaurs real? Were they fakes? The *Times* reporter was impressed. "If fakes," he wrote, "they were masterpieces."

## How Stop-Motion Got Its Start

The next day, Doyle revealed the truth. The movie was a hoax. The dinos were models made of steel, cotton, and rubber. The "Lost World" jungle in

Because of camera trickery, the small dinosaur model looks much larger than the actors in this shot.

the movie was also a model. How did the dinos move? That was Willis O'Brien's doing.

O'Brien used camera tricks to make the dinosaurs come alive. He shot the movie frame by frame. Before shooting each frame, he moved the models just a little bit. He did this again and again — more than a thousand

## Behind the Scenes:
### *Visual and Sound Effects*

In the film world, special effects are often called FX. Special effects can involve video or sound. VFX is a short way of referring to visual effects. SFX is short for sound effects.

times for each minute of film. When the separate frames were linked together, it looked like the dinos were moving on their own. This method is called stop-motion animation.

O'Brien had another trick up his sleeve. He filmed the dinos in close-up, so they looked big. Separately, he filmed actors from a distance, so they looked small. When he combined the shots, he had a single image with a large dino towering over its human prey.

## The Birth of Kong

O'Brien's camera tricks were a powerful tool. For the next seventy years, movie special effects relied on a similar mix of stop-motion animation and live-action shots.

In the early 1930s, O'Brien applied his VFX skills to a movie classic — the first *King Kong*. In one stop-motion sequence, he filmed Kong "climbing" the Empire State Building. The basic model of Kong was only 18 inches (46 centimeters) tall. The top of the "skyscraper" wasn't much bigger. But on the big screen, O'Brien made it look like the huge ape had reached the top of the world's tallest building. The filmmakers also made super-sized models of Kong's head, hand, and foot. Using the very large model of the ape's hand, O'Brien made it look like Kong was holding actress Fay Wray in his huge, hairy paw.

## Bringing Skeletons to Life

*King Kong* caught the eye of a thirteen-year old named Ray Harryhausen. The younger man spent much of the next twenty years trying to master O'Brien's methods. In 1949, he and O'Brien joined forces on another ape movie, *Mighty Joe Young*.

Back then, most science-fiction and fantasy flicks had low budgets. As a VFX artist, Harryhausen

## Behind the Scenes:
### *Faking It*

In most live-action movies, just about everything is fake. The characters feel real, but they're only actors. The fight wounds look real, but they're just makeup and ketchup. The spaceships seem real, but they're merely models. Does the script say it's a rainy day? Turn on the sprinklers. Want a tornado? Switch on the wind machine. Need a snowstorm? Cue the paper flakes, foam, and fake frost.

If nearly everything in most movies is fake already, what do we mean by special effects? Special effects in movies turn the art of fakery into a science. In VFX-driven movies, filmmakers use camera tricks to show scenes that could never happen in everyday life. Heroes battle with skeletons. Apes climb skyscrapers. People sprout extra arms and heads. Straight dramas use film fakery and make it look normal. VFX movies use film fakery and make it look — awesome!

# CELEBRITY SNAPSHOT

## Ray Harryhausen

**Born:** June 29, 1920, in Los Angeles, California

**Film Career:** VFX, producer, director

**Academy Awards:** Special award (1991)

**Top Films:** The 7th Voyage of Sinbad; Jason and the Argonauts; One Million Years B.C.; Clash of the Titans

**Backstory:** Harryhausen got his start making sci-fi movies. In several films, space aliens or monsters attacked major cities. He turned to the Sinbad story because he wanted to try something different. "I got tired of destroying cities," he says. "I destroyed Rome. I destroyed Washington. I destroyed New York. So I was looking for a way to use stop-motion that hadn't been used before."

Ray Harryhausen shows his Sinbad skeleton and sketches.

As the star of *Jason and the Argonauts*, actor Todd Armstrong "fought" an army of stop-motion skeletons in Harryhausen's VFX classic.

worked wonders with very little money. Made in 1958, *The 7th Voyage of Sinbad* was his first color movie. One stunning sequence showed Sinbad, a sailor, in a sword fight with a living skeleton. The scene used stop-motion animation to make the skeleton come alive.

In *Jason and the Argonauts*, Ray Harryhausen topped himself. The 1963 fantasy was based on a Greek myth. The high point of the film was a battle between seven skeletons and three real actors. The VFX master filmed the scene using a mix of stop-motion and live action. And he did it all without computers!

# CHAPTER 2

# Star Wars and Beyond

When George Lucas directed the first *Star Wars* film in the 1970s, he did more than make a movie. He created an industry.

### Big Dreams

Lucas was a shy, quiet guy with big dreams. He worked on the *Star Wars* script for two years. His script called for space aliens, robots, and a space station powerful enough to destroy a whole planet. The story had huge space battles and tremendous explosions.

Lucas knew what he wanted. But he lacked the technical skills to make it happen. To make *Star Wars*, he had to find skilled people willing to try new things. He formed a company called Industrial Light & Magic, or ILM. ILM did all the special effects for the film. It was the first true visual effects company in movie history. Many ILM pioneers have gone on to become top VFX artists on other films.

## A Camera Controlled by a Computer

Lucas studied films of real air battles. He saw how different combat aircraft moved in different patterns. He loved the way the cameras moved when filming the action. He wanted the space battles in *Star Wars* to have the same look. The problem was that he wasn't filming real aircraft. All his spaceships were just models. How could he make his models look like they were really speeding through space?

To solve this problem, Lucas turned to John Dykstra. Dykstra knew that by moving the camera in special ways, he could make it look like the spaceships were moving. His team at ILM built a

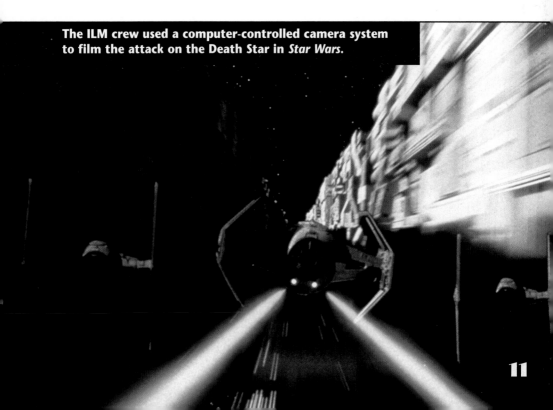

The ILM crew used a computer-controlled camera system to film the attack on the Death Star in *Star Wars*.

# CELEBRITY SNAPSHOT
## John Dykstra

**Born:** June 3, 1947, in Long Beach, California

**Film Career:** VFX

**Academy Awards:** For VFX for *Star Wars* (1977) and *Spider-Man 2* (2004)

**Other Top Films:** *Star Trek — The Motion Picture*; *Stuart Little*; *Spider-Man*

**Backstory:** Dykstra is a man of many skills. He studied industrial design. He was an expert model maker. He had worked as a photographer for famous rock bands. He knew how to fly airplanes.

Dykstra has fond memories of his early days with the *Star Wars* team at ILM. "We stayed there 24 hours a day," he recalled. "We lived and ate and slept that movie. . . . We had a really good time. It was very much a family."

VFX wizard John Dykstra holds the Oscar he won for *Star Wars*.

motion-control camera system. The system was connected to a computer. The computer told the camera exactly which way to go. The robot camera could shoot from under a model or above it. The camera could also tilt in different directions. Different views of different spacecraft could then be blended into a single shot.

Most of the models were very small. The robot camera shot them in close-up to make them look bigger. The models were also filmed in slow motion. When the film was shown at normal speed, it looked like they were moving very fast.

**Backgrounds and Blue Screen**

The robot camera solved part of the problem of faking flight. A method called blue screen solved the other part. A blue screen is a big screen filled with blue light. (Today, a green screen with green light is also used.)

ILM's Richard Edlund developed many of the blue-screen tricks used in *Star Wars*. First the camera filmed the actors or model ships in front of the blue screen. Then the right background replaced the blue in the shot.

Take a well-known scene in *Star Wars*. Han Solo and Chewbacca are in the cockpit of the *Millennium*

# CELEBRITY SNAPSHOT
## Richard Edlund

**Born:** December 6, 1940, in Fargo, North Dakota

**Film Career:** VFX

**Academy Awards:** For VFX on *Star Wars* (1977) and *Raiders of the Lost Ark* (1981); special awards in 1980, 1981, 1983, and 1986

**Other Top Films:** *The Empire Strikes Back*; *Poltergeist*; *Return of the Jedi*; *Ghostbusters*; *Die Hard*; *Air Force One*

**Backstory:** Like Dykstra, Edlund brought many skills to ILM. A mechanical engineer, he also knew art and photography. "If I needed to come up with some gadget," he says, "I could readily build it in an afternoon. . . . Every other day we were doing something that had never been done before. We had to invent ourselves out of problems all the time."

Richard Edlund made it look like Harrison Ford was barely escaping a runaway boulder in *Raiders of the Lost Ark*.

*Falcon.* As the spaceship makes the jump to light speed, we see the stars streak by in front of them. Of course, that's not how it looked to the actors. When the scene was filmed, they were sitting in front of a blue screen. The starry background was added later.

## Computer Graphics

ILM applied the tricks in *Star Wars* to later movies. In fact, blue screens and green screens are still widely used. Today, however, VFX artists have a powerful new tool. That tool is computer graphics.

Using the computer, ILM and other VFX shops can change a live-action shot. They can add things that look real but exist only in the digital world. For example, in *Star Wars: Episode II — Attack of the Clones*, Yoda is fully digital. Today, VFX artists can create digital characters, objects, and backgrounds. They can add their digital creations to any scene.

In 2004, director Kerry Conran made a movie called *Sky Captain and the World of Tomorrow.* The movie starred Jude Law, Gwyneth Paltrow, and Angelina Jolie. The actors were real. But everything else in the film was digital. The actors performed all their scenes in front of a blue screen. Conran did everything else on his computer.

# Stunt Work

Have you seen any of the *James Bond* movies? All the 007 films feature fast-paced chases on almost anything people can ride, drive, sail, or fly. Visual effects create much of the excitement. Great stunts are also part of the show.

Movie stunt artists plunge through windows, leap from bridges, and run through raging fires. They dangle from helicopters and crash cars at breakneck speeds. A few top stars do their own stunts. Others use a stunt double. The crashes, fires, and explosions you see in movies are carefully planned and controlled. Even so, stunt work is risky. Stunt artists sometimes get hurt.

### Skills, Thrills, and Spills

Great stunt work helped make *Ben-Hur* a movie masterpiece. This 1959 film won eleven Oscars, including best picture. The most thrilling scene in

# CELEBRITY SNAPSHOT
## Debbie Evans

**Born:** February 5, 1958, in Lakewood, California

**Film Career:** Stunts, actress

**Top Films:** *The Fast and the Furious; The Matrix Reloaded*

**Backstory:** Debbie Evans is one of the top stunt drivers in Hollywood. She began riding a motorcycle when she was only six years old. By her teens, she was doing cycle stunts in TV and movies. More recently, she won awards for being a stunt double for Michelle Rodriguez and Carrie-Anne Moss. In 2003, she entered the Motorcycle Hall of Fame.

**Debbie Evans (left) poses with her sister Donna, also a stuntwoman, at the Taurus World Stunt Awards in 2005.**

**For the motorcycle stunts in *The Matrix Reloaded*, Debbie Evans doubled for Carrie-Anne Moss.**

# Behind the Scenes:
## *Awards for Special Effects and Stunts*

The first Academy Award for special effects was given in 1938. It covered special effects of all types. In 1963, the Academy began giving separate Oscars for visual effects and sound effects. The Academy of Science Fiction, Fantasy & Horror Films hands out the Saturn Awards. These awards honor the year's best sci-fi, fantasy, and horror movies. Films also compete for annual awards from the Visual Effects Society.

There is no Oscar for stunts. The Taurus World Stunt Awards have been given each year since 2001. Honors include best fight, best stunt using fire, best high stunt, and best vehicle stunt.

the movie is a chariot race. The scene was shot with real actors, horses, and chariots. It uses few of the tools VFX artists now depend on.

Charlton Heston, star of *Ben-Hur*, spent five weeks learning to drive a chariot. For the most dangerous shots, he had a stunt double — Joe Canutt. Heston later called Joe the greatest natural athlete he had ever seen.

Many hours were spent planning each stunt. The filmmakers worked hard to make sure no one got hurt. Even so, disaster nearly happened. While driving Heston's chariot at top speed, Canutt was tossed in midair. Somehow, he grabbed the front rail of the chariot, did a handstand, and threw himself clear. Otherwise, he could have been crushed under the heavy vehicle.

The race was shot from many different angles. One camera was high above the crowd. Another filmed the race from a moving car in front of the horses. Other cameras were in fixed positions at ground level. In the finished film, cuts are quick. The movie shifts rapidly between wide shots of the whole race and close-ups of the drivers, horses, and chariot wheels. The fast cutting adds to the excitement.

This scene had tremendous impact on makers of action films. Many directors — including George Lucas — studied it in film school. Lucas based the pod race in *Star Wars: Episode I — The Phantom Menace* on the chariot race in *Ben-Hur*.

**The chariot race in *Ben-Hur* marked a turning point in the history of movie stunts.**

## Staging a Fall

Imagine that you're a movie director. You're making a movie in which the hero chases a villain across the rooftop of a tall building. While trying to escape, the villain trips and plunges off the roof to the street below. What special effects and stunts would you use to shoot your scene? How can you make the scene look real while making sure that no one gets hurt?

You might start by filming on an actual rooftop. These first shots are filmed safely away from the edge of the roof. Next, you could build a set that looks like the rooftop. It needs to be on a platform, perhaps 10 feet (3 meters) off the ground. The camera shows the villain — or his stunt double — plunging over the edge of the roof. What the camera doesn't show is the stunt artist falling safely onto a mattress at the base of the set.

The next shot is taken from a distance. It shows a body falling from the roof to the street. For this shot, you could use a dummy that looks like the villain. Or you could use computer graphics. The final shot shows the actor lying in the street. For this shot, makeup and fake blood make it look like the villain is dead or injured.

# Fighting Hard, Flying High

# CHAPTER 4

Fighting has always been a big part of movies. War films have huge battles. Westerns have bar brawls and shootouts. Horror flicks have violent struggles with psychos, monsters, and zombies. Movie fights are terrific crowd pleasers. They're also a great way for stunt artists to show their skills.

Movie fights are carefully rehearsed. Each move the fighters make is planned in advance. To keep from getting hurt — and to avoid hurting others — stunt fighters need great body control. The right props can also prevent injuries. For example, windows in fight scenes aren't made of real glass. They use a plastic material called breakaway glass, which is much safer.

## Just for Kicks

Some of the best fight movies come from China. Since the 1960s, martial-arts movies from Hong

## Behind the Scenes:
### So You Want to Do Hollywood Stunts . . .?

There's no easy way to learn Hollywood stunts. Movie stunts are much too dangerous to practice at home. The best thing you can do is to get in shape. Practice hard at sports. Ride a horse, a bike, or a skateboard. Learn gymnastics. Take martial-arts classes.

Training as an actor is also helpful. Get as much stage experience as you can. When you're ready to jump into stunt work, several private groups run classes, workshops, and stunt schools.

Kong have become popular around the world. The biggest martial-arts star was Bruce Lee. By his late teens, he was a martial-arts master. His feet and fists were lightning fast. He had a hard time getting work in Hollywood. But back in Asia, he landed a starring role in *The Big Boss*. The 1971 film — also called *Fists of Fury* — became the most popular movie in Asia up to that time. Bruce Lee died in his early thirties.

The next Hong Kong movie superstar was Jackie Chan. Chan is a gifted comic actor who likes to do his own stunts. He continues to make movies in Asia as well as Hollywood. Other stars of martial-arts movies include Jet Li from *Fearless* and Zhang Ziyi from *House of Flying Daggers*.

## Defying Gravity

If you've seen *Crouching Tiger, Hidden Dragon*, you'll remember this scene. Zhang Ziyi (as Jen Yu) is fighting some thugs on the upper floor of a Chinese inn. Sword in hand, she backflips her way down a flight of steps. On the lower level, Monk Jing confronts her. "Who are you?" he demands. Responding to his challenge, she twirls rapidly in the air while rising up to the balcony. Then she crosses swords with more thugs before making a double somersault through the air down to his level. "I am," she says, "the Invincible Sword Goddess!"

The *Matrix* trilogy also has scenes that defy gravity. That's no accident. The same fight director

**Zhang Ziyi's fists and feet fly in** *Crouching Tiger, Hidden Dragon.*

# CELEBRITY SNAPSHOT
## Yuen Wo Ping

**Born:** 1945 in Guangzhou, China

**Film Career:** Action director, actor, writer

**Top Films:** *Iron Monkey; the Matrix trilogy; Crouching Tiger, Hidden Dragon; Kill Bill: Vol. 2*

**Backstory:** "When we make an action movie in Hong Kong," Yuen says, "we like to use actors who can fight. That's always easier." When he started work on *The Matrix*, he was worried. "When I saw the actors could not punch or kick properly, I got dizzy," he recalls. The stars needed four months of training. Only then were they ready to do some of their own *Matrix* stunts.

**Yuen Wo Ping (right) discusses a fight scene with *Crouching Tiger* director Ang Lee.**

Hidden wires boost Keanu Reeves (left) and
Hugo Weaving in this *Matrix* fight scene.

who worked on *Crouching Tiger* also worked on the
*Matrix* movies. Yuen Wo Ping developed the art of
wire stunts in Hong Kong.

## All Wired Up

For wire stunts, hooks are hidden in the actors'
costumes. Wires or cables are then passed through
the hooks. During the stunt, you see the actors
rising into the air or soaring across rooftops. What
you don't see are the crew members holding the
wires that guide each actor's flight. All traces of the
wires are covered up later, when the film is edited.

Many hours go into planning and rehearsing wire
stunts. The actors must learn how to control their
bodies as they move. When a wire stunt is done
well, it can look as graceful as ballet.

# CHAPTER 5

# *Superheroes*

Superman, Batman, and Spider-Man battle evildoers. They have secret identities. They draw on unusual powers. And that's not all they have in common. All three superheroes started out in comic books. Each had his own TV series. Finally, each made the leap to movies, DVDs, and video games. The result — super profits.

## FX Challenges

It's easy to see why comic-book heroes have become so common in movies. Their powers — and those of their enemies — give VFX wizards and stunt artists a chance to shine. The makers of *Spider-Man 2* had great fun showing the web-spinner swinging from building to building. They combined live-action shots in front of blue screens with computer graphics to make Spidey soar. Even more challenging was the creation of Spidey's enemy — Doc Ock. Ock has four snaky mechanical arms attached to his back. The VFX

# CELEBRITY SNAPSHOT
## Stan Lee

**Born:** December 28, 1922, in New York City

**Film Career:** Writer, producer

**Top Films:** *The Spider-Man* and *X-Men* series

**Backstory:** With Marvel Comics, Lee helped to create the Fantastic Four, Incredible Hulk, X-Men, and Spider-Man. When the first *Spider-Man* film appeared in 2002, he wrote an article explaining why Spidey is still so popular. Lee pointed out that Spider-Man isn't always certain he's doing the right thing. "Sometimes the villains aren't all bad and the good guys aren't all good," he wrote.

**Actor Alfred Molina (right) and a team of VFX wizards helped Doc Ock make the leap from Stan Lee's comic books to the big screen in *Spider-Man 2*.**

## Behind the Scenes:
*Filmmakers and Gamers*

People in the film business take the link between action movies and video games very seriously. U.S. sales of all video games and game systems now total more than $10 billion a year. Many young actors, directors, and VFX artists are gamers. The voices of Samuel L. Jackson, Michelle Rodriguez, and Vin Diesel have been featured on recent games. John Singleton is a film director who has also worked on video-game design. "I've grown up with a joystick in my hand," he says.

artists used robots, puppets, and computer graphics to make the villain's arms look real.

For many years, white males dominated the world of VFX, stunts, and superheroes. That pattern is changing. In the gory *Blade* series, for example, Wesley Snipes — an African American actor — stars as a vampire hunter. In the *X-Men* films, the characters are as varied as their powers. For example, Phoenix, played by Famke Janssen, can move objects with her mind. As portrayed by Halle Berry, Storm can control the weather. One touch

As the vampire-hunting hero of *Blade: Trinity*, Wesley Snipes battles an army of the undead.

from Anna Paquin's character Rogue can suck the life force out of anyone.

Casting men and women of different ages, sizes, and colors as superheroes opens up more roles for actors. It also creates more chances for the stunt artists who work along with them. VFX shops, too, are seeking talented people from different backgrounds. "The cream will always rise to the top," says one industry expert. "If you're good at what you do, you'll stand out and always find work."

*The Chronicles of Narnia: The Lion, the Witch and the Wardrobe* earned an Oscar nomination for its magical visual effects.

# Glossary

**Academy Award** — also called an Oscar; an award given out by the movie industry.

**backstory** — the background story to something seen on screen.

**digital** — created by computer.

**director** — the person who controls the creative part of making a movie.

**frame** — the separate photographs that make up a movie; also, the boundary that separates what can be seen on screen from what cannot.

**ILM** — short for Industrial Light & Magic, the special-effects company formed to make *Star Wars*.

**industrial design** — the art of developing products and improving their appearance and usefulness.

**invincible** — cannot be beaten.

**prop** — a movable object used in a scene.

**set** — scenery built for use in a movie or play.

**stunt double** — a stunt artist who stands in for an actor who is unwilling or unable to do a particular stunt.

**trilogy** — a three-part series.

**VFX** — short for visual effects.

# To Find Out More

## Books

*Movie Science: 40 Mind-Expanding, Reality-Bending, Starstruck Activities for Kids.* Jim Wiese (Jossey-Bass)

*Special Effects.* Jake Hamilton (DK Publishing)

*Special Effects.* On the Edge (series). Christopher Richardson (Chelsea House Publications)

*Special Effects: An Introduction to Movie Magic.* Ron Miller (Twenty-First Century Books)

*Stunt Double.* High Interest Books (series). Aileen Weintraub (Children's Press)

## Videos

*Ben-Hur* (Warner Home Video) G

*Crouching Tiger, Hidden Dragon* (Sony) PG-13

*The 7th Voyage of Sinbad* (Sony) G

*Spider-Man 2* (Sony) PG-13

## Web Sites

Industrial Light & Magic
*www.ilm.com*
See movies on how *Star Wars* special effects were created

NOVA Online: Special Effects: Attack of the 50-Foot Chicken
*www.pbs.org/wgbh/nova/specialfx2/green.html*
Pretend to be a special effects supervisor for a movie

**Publisher's note to educators and parents:** Our editors have carefully reviewed these Web sites to ensure that they are suitable for children. Many Web sites change frequently, however, and we cannot guarantee that a site's future contents will continue to meet our high standards of quality and educational value. Be advised that children should be closely supervised whenever they access the Internet.

# Index

**32**

### About the Author

Geoffrey M. Horn has been a fan of music, movies, and sports for as long as he can remember. He has written more than three dozen books for young people and adults, along with hundreds of articles for encyclopedias and other works. He lives in southwestern Virginia, in the foothills of the Blue Ridge Mountains, with his wife, their collie, and four cats. He dedicates this book to Leona, Melissa, and Alan Davidson.